Reflections...

Timeless Wisdom for
Challenging Times

By William E. McEwen II

To Marci:
Thanks for being here
today and for your Contribution
to our CLASS.
Hope you enjoy this
book. My Best, Sept.
Bill 2012

Dedicated to:

This book is dedicated to my children Will, Clark, and Honey, to my grandchildren, and to all those future generations yet unborn. I dedicate any wisdom that may arise from this book to them; may it be of some value in their life.

Foreword

*I met William (Bill) McEwen in 1992 at a
workshop in New York where I was facilitating
for the former Covey Leadership Center. At the
time I was Co-Founder and President of the
Covey Education Division. Little did I know
then, that this workshop would be the
beginning of a great life- long friendship. Bill
McEwen is one of my best friends.*

*Bill McEwen grew up in Duck River, Tennessee.
For those of you who may not know, Duck River
is about sixty miles southwest of Nashville just
off the Natchez Trace Parkway. He has lived
there all of his life, right next to his home place,
where his brother Jim lives. Bill went to college,
served in Viet Nam and came back home to
raise a family. Bill has two wonderful
daughters Honey and Clark and a great son
Will.*

*When I think of Bill's life and when I read this
book, I think of the following quote by* <u>*Leon
Joseph Cardinal Suenens*</u>*:*

"Happy are those that dream dreams and are ready to pay the price to make them come true."

Bill McEwen knows what it means to be "Happy". He has paid the price. If one would pull up in the drive way of his farm in Duck River, and see the peacocks, hear the dogs bark, and see the simple log cabin that he and his sweetheart Shirley run as Bed and Breakfast, you might think, this is a simple man living a simple life. But after meeting Bill and listening to his great wisdom, you soon learn his depths are only reached through enlightenment and a complex understanding of the world around him. Truly, "Simplicity on the far side of Complexity."

As you read this journey of Bill's life, enjoy, reflect, and perhaps take another step toward your own enlightenment.

Chuck Farnsworth
Sarasota, Florida

Introduction

Fill your bowl to the brim
And it will spill.
Keep sharpening your knife
And it will blunt.
Chase after money and security
And you heart will never unclench.
Care about people's approval
And you will be their prisoner.

Do your work, then step back
The only path to serenity.

Tao Te Ching (Verse 9)

For a number of years this collection laid dormant, patiently waiting to be shared. Timing plays a big role in all our lives, and writing this book was no exception. King Solomon writing some 3,000 years ago captured the essence of my thoughts about timing when he said: "There is a time for everything and a season for every activity under heaven". This is my season to write, to share, "and to step back".

Since my official retirement in December of 2007, I have had no schedule, no agenda, and "no shoulds". I've read extensively, taught some classes and workshops, mediated regularly, practiced my Qi Gong, and spent much time enjoying nature and appreciating this special place I call home... which I fondly refer to sometimes as "my briar patch". A lot of things have gotten digested during this completely open and uncharted time. Without a doubt, it has been the most mentally, physically, emotionally, and spiritually inspiring time of my life.

This collection began in 1960 when I was a freshman at the University of Tennessee in Knoxville and has continued to the present. Having been an avid and diverse reader for most of my life, I simply began to capture phrases and quotes which at the time resonated with me. In addition, I've had the opportunity to meet many interesting and wonderful individuals who have also shared their insights. And if, by chance, that I'm able to see a bit further down the road it is simply because I've stood on their shoulders.

I do not remember or at the time, simply failed to note the source for some of this material, and I accept full responsibility for this. However, this book is not intended for publication, only as a gift. If individuals find some meaning and value on these pages, I encourage them to pass on their insights and share with their family and friends.

I have not attempted to organize this content by subject; rather it is chronological and will hopefully reflect my own personal journey. The careful reader will come to understand that these words reflect many of the things which have been and are important in my life. In essence, they reflect some of my values, perceptions, and philosophy.

This is not a book to be read from cover to cover in one sitting. I suggest living with it, picking it up frequently, and reflecting on the wisdom. In doing so, please remember that the words are no more than signposts which can lead you, the reader, to your own deeper reality. Allow the book to do its work, to challenge you and perhaps awaken you from some of your old ways of repetitive and conditioned thinking.

It is my hope that these diverse quotations will serve as an invitation to take this wisdom deeply into your own hearts and minds. It has been my intent in offering this compilation that you might find encouragement and illumination as you follow your own path toward more sanity and deeper wisdom. Finally, as Sandra Knell once said, "I am looking forward to looking back on all this."

I am a part of all that I have met

Tennyson

Gather ye Rosebuds while ye may
Old time is still a flying
For that same flower that smiles today
Tomorrow might be dying

Robert Herrick

What though thy Radiance which was once so bright, be now forever taken from my sight. Though nothing can bring back the hour of Splendor is the Grass, of Glory in the flower. I will grieve not, rather find, strength in what remains behind.

Wordsworth

Most of life's problems are like those interchanges we find on our highways: unlikely though it may seem, there is a way out

Bell McClure Syndicate

There is only one danger I find in life; you may take to many precautions

"The Goal"

To love is to stop comparing

Unknown

When a thing is funny, search it for a hidden truth

George Bernard Shaw

We can easily forgive a child who is afraid of the dark; the real tragedy of life is when men are afraid of the light

Plato

A man who is not afraid to roll up his sleeves seldom loses his shirt

Unknown

No man can command until he has first learned to obey

Aristotle

When elephants fight the grass is sure to be trampled

> *Hindu Proverb*

They were not stupid, they were not biased, but they were wrong

> *Abraham Lincoln*

The purpose for which a thing exists gives one the truth about the object; look ahead and discover for what purpose the object was created, and one can discover the secret of that object

> *Aristotle*

We can only find out what we are by finding out where we are going

> *Aristotle*

When men build on false grounds, the more they build the greater the error

> *Aristotle*

Happy indeed is the man who knows his own limitations

Unknown

All that tread the globe are but a handful to the tribes that slumber in its bosom

William Cullen Bryant

Lone, wandering, but not lost...

William Cullen Bryant

Trust thy self; every heart vibrates to that iron string

Emerson

When faith is lost, when honor dies, the man is dead

Robert G. Whittier

We never know how high we are till we are called to rise; and then if we are true to plan, our statues touch the skies

Emily Dickinson

As imperceptibly as grief the summer lapsed away

> *Emily Dickinson*

A man's character and his garden both reflect the amount of weeding that was done during the growing season

> *"Houston Post"*

When schemes are laid in advance, it is surprising how often the circumstances fit in with them

> *Sir William Oliver*

The essence of virtue is moderation

> *Aristotle*

Nature's first green is gold, her hardest hue to hold. Her early leaf's a flower, but only so an hour. Then leaf subsides to leaf. So Eden sank to grief; so dawn goes down today. Nothing gold can stay

> *Robert Frost*

The mass of men lead lives of quiet desperation. The man who goes alone can start today; but he who travels with another must wait till that other is ready, and it may be a long time before they get off. Be it life or death, we crave only reality. Time is but the stream I go fishing in. I drink of it; but while I drink I see the sandy bottom and detect how shallow it is. Its thin current slides away, but eternity remains. If a man does not keep pace with his companions, perhaps it is because he hears a different drummer. Let him step to the music he hears, however measured or far away

Thoreau

Come forth into the light of things; Let nature be your teacher

Henry Wordsworth

The evil that men do lives after them; the good is often interred with their bones

Shakespeare

All the world's a stage, and all men and women merely players. They have their exits and entrances, and one man in his time plays many parts

> *Shakespeare*

Life's but a walking shadow, a poor player that struts and frets his hour upon the stage and then is heard no more

> *Shakespeare*

Religion is a sum of scruples which impede the free exercise of our faculties

> *Soloman Reinach*

Our birth is but a sleep and a forgetting

> *Henry Wordsworth*

The glorious lamp of heaven, the sun
The higher he's a-getting
The sooner will his race be run
And nearer he's to setting

> *Robert Herrick*

A thing of beauty is a joy forever; its loveliness increases

Keats

Success is counted sweetest by those who never succeed

Emily Dickinson

Hope is the thing with feathers that perches in the soul and sings the tune without the words and never stops at all

Emily Dickinson

No man is an island. Every man is a piece of the continent, a part of the main

John Donne

The corrupt of the best is the worst

Aristotle

Life is tons of discipline

Robert Frost

Those who complain about the way the ball bounces are usually the ones who dropped it

Unknown

Religion means the feelings, acts, and experiences of individual men in their solitude; so far as they apprehend themselves to stand in relation to whatever they may consider the divine

William James

The essence of religion is the personal encounter between God and man

H. Farmer

Religion provides an illusory happiness...it is the opium of the poor...the idea of God is the keystone of a perverted civilization

Karl Marx

Man, by nature, is a political animal

Aristotle

Religion is self-commitment to what one holds to be the source of all human good

H. Wieman

One cannot step down into the same river twice

C.E. Carrington

There is nothing more harmful in the world than a theory killed by a fact

C.E. Carrington

Every organ contains within itself the seeds of its own decay

Plato

All power corrupts, and absolute power corrupts absolutely

Lord Acton

Man is the measure of all things

Heracleitus

A man who lives alone must be either a God or a beast

Aristotle

Such great evils have been brought upon the world by religions

Unknown

I have fought a good fight, I have finished my course, I have kept the faith

The Bible (Timothy)

Man is born free; and everywhere he is in chains

Rousseau

The tissue of life to be
We weave with colors all our own
And in the field of destiny
We reap as we have sown

John G.Whitter

Gratitude is the memory of the heart

Unknown

He who receives a benefit with gratitude repays the first installment on his debt

Unknown

War always raises more questions than it solves

Unknown

It is love which moves the sun and the other stars

Dante

Words are wise men's countenance but are the money of fools

Thomas Hobbs

Don't do unto others what you don't want others to do to you

Confucius

I sometimes shrink at evils recollected and sometimes start at evils anticipated

Samuel Johnson

Poetry is the first and last of all knowledge. It is as immortal as the heart of man. Poetry is the spontaneous overflow of powerful feelings

Wordsworth

St. Agnes Eve...Ah bitter chill it was
The owl, all its feathers, was a cold
The hare limped trembling through the frozen grass
And silent was the flock in wooly fold

Keats

Life, like the dome of a many colored glass, stains the white radiance of eternity until death tramples it to fragments

Shelley

The old order changes yielding place to the new, and God fulfills himself in many ways

Tennyson

I hold it true whatever befalls
I feel it when I sorrow most
It's better to have loved and lost
Than never to have loved at all

Tennyson

So live, that when thou summons comes to join the innumerable caravan, which moves to that mysterious realm, where each shall take his chamber in the silent halls of death, thou go not like the quarry slave at night scourged to his dungeon, but, sustained and soothed by an unfaltering trust, approach thy grave like one who wraps the drapery of his couch about him and lies down to pleasant dreams

Bryant

A man's reach should exceed his grasp
                                    Robert Browning

Shall life succeed in that it seems to fail?
                                    Robert Browning

*There is no odor as bad as that which arises
from goodness tainted*
                                        Thoreau

Be it life or death, we crave only reality
                                        Thoreau

*No way of thinking or doing, however
ancient, can be trusted without proof*
                                        Thoreau

Nothing can bring you peace but yourself
                                        Emerson

*The ultimate sin of the mind is the failure to
pay enough attention*
                                        Unknown

Life can only be understood backward, but it must be lived forward

> *Unknown*

The only man worth envying is the one who has found a cause bigger than himself

> *Unknown*

Life leaps like a geyser for those who drill through the rock of inertia

> *Unknown*

The political party that gets the credit when the sun shines also gets the blame for the rain

> *Eric Goldman*

Nothing is worse than war?
Dishonor is worse than war
Slavery is worse than war

> *Winston Churchill*

If we cannot now end our differences, at least we can help make the world safe for diversity. For, in the final analysis, our most common basic link is that we all inhabit this small planet. We all breathe the same air. We all cherish our children's future. And we are all mortal

Unknown

He who forgets the lessons of history must relive his mistakes again

Unknown

Those who make peaceful revolution impossible will make violent revolution inevitable

John F. Kennedy

You can tell the size of a man by what makes him mad

Will Rogers

Democracies which are fundamentally peaceful have to receive external stimuli to force them to re-arm. They do not have a long range point of view .The dictatorship with its long range policy can always keep ahead of the democracy

"Why England Slept"

And when he fell in a whirlwind
He went down
As when a lordly cedar, green with boughs
Goes down with a great shout upon the hills
And leaves a lonesome place against the sky

Edwin Markham

Nobody is as big as he thinks he is or so small as his enemies are sure

Unknown

The difficult we do immediately, but the impossible takes a little time

Unknown

It strikes me as time goes on how something funny, even farcical, can suddenly without any apparent reason, break up into something gloomy and tragic. Sometimes it seems as if life is being manipulated just to confuse us

Bill McEwen

We have got to understand that all our lives the danger, the uncertainty, the need for alertness, for discipline, for effort, will be upon us

Unknown

The civilizations that flourished and died in the past had opportunities for a limited period of time to change the course of history. Sooner or later, however, they passed the point of no return and the decisions were no longer theirs to make

William Knowland

Over the centuries more than one powerful nation has out of meanness and shortsightedness, tried to walk against a great tide of human aspirations and been swallowed ignominiously

Eric Goldman

The present is our own. The future is only promised to us, but the past belongs to itself

Robert E. Lee

For when the one great scorer comes to write against your name, he marks not that you won or lost, but how you played the game

Grantland Rice

The chief purpose of an education is to train the mind and the will to do what ought to be done, when it ought to be done, whether you want to do it or not

Unknown

Man is born to act; to act is to affirm the worth of an end; and to affirm the worth of an end is to create an ideal

Oliver W. Holmes

Life is unfair. Some people are sick and others are well. Some live and some die. There is always inequity in life

John F. Kennedy

We know from the past some of the things we will do. We will make mistakes; we always have. But from our beginning, in hindsight at least, our social direction is clear. We have moved to become one people out of many. We have failed sometimes, taken wrong paths, paused for renewal, filled our bellies and licked our wounds, but we have never slipped back... never

John Steinbeck

A dying people tolerate the present, reject the future, and find its satisfaction in past greatness and half remembered glory

Unknown

The only people who never make mistakes are those who never do anything

Loyd Morris

A hundred times a day I remind myself that my inner and outer life depend on the labors of other men, living and dead, and that I must exert myself in order to give in the same measure that I have received

Albert Einstein

The truly extraordinary man is truly the ordinary man

Unknown

We must not allow ourselves to be trapped in the backwash of a stagnant stream

Unknown

In almost any subject, your passion for the subject will save you. If you only care enough for a result, you most certainly will attain it

William James

The chief task of the writer is, above all, to make the reader see

Joseph Conrad

The palest ink is better than the most retentive memory

Chinese Proverb

Reading is to the mind what exercise is to the body

Unknown

The hottest places in hell are reserved for those, who in a time of crisis, maintain their neutrality

Dante

If I have succeeded in my inquiries more than others, I owe it less to any superior strength of mind, than to a habit of patient thinking

Isaac Newton

A speech is like a love affair. Any fool can start it but to end it requires considerable skill

Mancroft

Three organizational myths: people who have been there the longest are the smartest; people who have the highest positions are the smartest; everything that I'm working on is important

Harry Brittan

We few, we happy few, we band of brothers; for he today who sheds his blood with me shall be my brother

Henry V

The worm shall feed sweetly on him, and he shall no longer be remembered
> *The Bible (Job)*

The years flow by like water. And one day men come home again
> *Thomas Wolfe*

His enemy was time. Or perhaps it was his friend. One never knows for sure
> *Thomas Wolfe*

Do not follow where the path may lead, instead go where there is no path and leave a trail
> *Unknown*

The greatest discovery in our generation is the discovery that human beings, by changing the inner attitude of their minds, can change the outer attitudes of their lives
> *William James*

He who knows others is wise; he who knows himself is enlightened

Lao-Tzu

Our remedies oft in ourselves do lie

William Shakespeare

There is only one corner of the universe that you can be certain of improving and that's your own self

Aldous Huxley

Go to your bosom; knock there and ask your heart what it doth know

William Shakespeare

In nature there are neither punishments nor rewards. There are only consequences

Chinese Proverb

Never be afraid to tread the path alone. Know which is your path and follow it wherever it may lead you

Unknown

Be a lamp unto yourself. Hold to the truth within you

The Buddha

Close your eyes and you will see clearly. Cease to listen and you will hear the truth. Be silent and your heart will sing.

Lao-Tzu

There are no atheists in foxholes

Unknown

When you come to the edge of all you have known, one of two things will happen: either you will step onto solid ground or you will learn how to fly

Unknown

I am a man of faith. My reliance is solely on God. One step is enough for me. The next step he will show me when the time for it comes

Gandhi

I have fought a good fight. I have finished my course. I have kept the faith

II Timothy 4:7

Repeat three times every day and then listen: Lord what would thou have me do today

Edgar Cayce

Cast thy bread upon the waters for thou shall find it after many days

Ecclesiastes 11:1

A man cannot be comfortable without his own approval

Mark Twain

The old law "an eye for an eye" leaves everybody blind. Hatred is not diminished by hatred at any time. Hatred is diminished by love. This is an eternal law

The Buddha

He who has a "why" to live for can bear with almost any "how"

Nietzsche

A gem is not polished without rubbing nor a man perfected without trials

Confucius

The only way to heal the pain is to embrace the pain

Fritz Perls

Do not store up for yourselves treasures on earth where moth and rust destroy and where thieves consume...

Mathew 6:20

But those who hope in the Lord will renew their strength. They will soar on wings like eagles; they will run and not grow weary...
Isaiah 40:31

In due season we shall reap if we faint not...
Galatians 6:9

To everything there is a season and a time to every purpose under heaven...
Ecclesiastes 3:1

Life only demands from you the strength that you possess. Only one feat is possible: not to have run away
Dag Hammarskjöld

Enlightenment begins on the other side of despair
Sartre

We are born into the world of nature; our second birth is into the world of spirit
                                    Bhagavad-Gita

I will forgive all things today
                                    A Course in Miracles

Man's main task in life is to give birth to himself, to become what he potentially is
                                    Eric Fromm

To be a traveler on this earth, you must know how to die and come to life again
                                    Goethe

I've lost my mind but I've come to my senses
                                    Bill McEwen

The greatest truths are simple and so are the greatest men
                                    Augustus and Julius Hare

When you have a disease do not try to find a cure. Find your center and you will be cured

> *Unknown*

Some things can be sensed, not explained

> *Bill McEwen*

The hottest places in hell are reserved for those, who in a time of crisis, maintain their neutrality

> *Dante*

Hemingway's definition of courage: "grace under pressure"

> *Ernest Hemingway*

There are few things wholly evil or wholly good

> *Abraham Lincoln*

I have yet to see a genius or a hero who, if struck by a burning match, would feel less pain than his undistinguished average brother...I see nothing offensive in the conception of fertilizer as the symbol of man's destiny...it is fertilizer that produces wheat and roses

Ayn Rand ("The Fountainhead")

All that we remember is your living face and that we loved you for being of our clay and spirit

David D. Duncan (Khe Sanh 1968)

Chasing yesterdays is a bum show, and if you have to prove it go back to your old front

Ernest Hemingway

Un-common valor was a common virtue

Marines at Khe Sanh (Jan.-Mar.'68)

The battlefield is a world of final simplicity
                    David D. Duncan ("I Protest")

War brings men down to beasts, quicker than whiskey, surer than women, and deadlier than money
                            William Allen White

What history and experience teach is this: that people and governments have never learned anything from history or acted on principles deduced from it
                                    Hegel

A private individual may do anything except that which is legally forbidden. A government official may do nothing except that which is legally permitted
        Ayn Rand ("The Objectivist Newsletter")

I believe that man will not merely endure, he will prevail. He is immortal not because he alone among creatures has an inexhaustible voice but because he has a soul, a spirit capable of compassion, sacrifice, and endurance

William Faulkner

Curves make the fastball look good

Unknown

It's really different now. I may hunt all day for one or two coveys...not too bad considering how the territory and the times have changed. If I put three or four birds in my vest, I figure that I've done alright. But I stay with it, year after year, keeping the dogs and waiting for November. Just because it's different doesn't mean it's not worth doing

Bill McEwen on Quail Hunting

Yesterday is gone; tomorrow may never come; now is the appointed time

Unknown

We do not know a nation until we know its pleasures, just as we do not know a man until we know how he spends his leisure

Lin Yutang

If you want inner peace find it in solitude, not speed, and if you would find yourself, look to the land from which you came and to which you go

Stewart Udall ("The Quiet Crisis")

It is amazing how few people are conscious of the importance of lying in bed

Lin Yutang

Nothing exists long when its time is past. Material wealth is only important to the small of mind. The important thing is to do the best with what one has. To each of us is given a life. To live with honor and pass on having left our mark; it is only essential that we do our part and leave our children strong

Louis Amour ("Flint")

A man who doesn't give a damn always has the edge

Louis Amour ("Flint")

In the end, one only experiences oneself

Nietzsche

There's nothing on earth so valuable as time, and there's nothing on earth as satisfying as the earth. Men of earth must use their wits to make time

John Bailey's Three Eternal Truths

A drink whether it be wine, beer, or whiskey is enjoyable, and it is one of life's greatest pleasures. Moderation is the key; I've found the following guidelines to be helpful:

1. Never drink before 5:00pm; one hour before dinner is my preference

2. Never drink after dinner

3. Never mix good whiskey/bourbon with anything except ice...or maybe a "little" water

4. Refrain from any alcoholic beverages for one month out of the year

Bill McEwen

In the spinning of planets and the march of suns, in the centuries and the millennium of time, one man is a small thing and does not matter very much. It is how a man lives and dies that matters. A man can live proudly and he can die proudly

Unknown

It is not enough to be busy. The question is what are we busy about

Thoreau

It is better to live one day as a lion than a dozen years as a sheep

Louis Amour ("Flint")

The experience taught me a few things: one is to listen to your gut, no matter how good something looks on paper. The second is that you're usually better off sticking with what you know, and the third is your best investments are sometimes the ones you don't make

Donald Trump ("Trump")

Teach as little as possible. When you teach someone, you deprive him of the ability to learn

Bill McEwen

This we know. The earth does not belong to us; we belong to the earth. Whatever befalls the earth befalls the sons and daughters of the earth. Humans do not weave the web of life; we are merely a strand in it. Whatever we do to the web we do to ourselves

Chief Seattle

When Mt. Everest was scaled, the phrase commonly used in the West to describe the feat "was the conquest of Everest". An Oriental whose writings have been deeply influenced by Taoism remarked:"We would put the matter differently. We would speak of befriending Everest".

Houston Smith ("The Religions of Man")

It is the marriage of the soul with nature that makes the intellect fruitful, which gives birth to the imagination

Thoreau ("The Journal")

There are no road maps to self discovery, no on ramps, no neon signs. It is a journey that begins by looking outward for insight and revelation, and winds up as an adventure within ourselves, bound for answers we had all along

Outward Bound Magazine

A good man is hard to understand. A son of a bitch always goes by the rules. I do not know all about a man until I have seen him cry; sooner or later you will see every man cry. It is like chemistry. When he cries he is separated into his component parts

Ernest Hemingway

Life for him was an adventure, perilous indeed, but men are not made for safe havens

Edith Hamilton (The Greek's Way)

You cannot harvest the lessons of your life except in aloneness

Unknown

Count no man successful until the day of his death. The only thing that a man can do successfully is to die

Unknown

One of the greatest gifts you can give another person is your attention

Bill McEwen

To live is to suffer; to survive is to find meaning in the suffering. If there is a purpose in life at all, there must be a purpose in living and dying. But no man can tell another what that purpose is. Each must find out for himself and must accept the responsibility that his answer prescribes

Victor Frankel

Do good, avoid evil, purify your mind
                              Buddhist Golden Rule

We bring a lot of rules to the system which don't need to be there
                              Bill McEwen

We make the road by walking it
                              Unknown

One ought every day at least, to hear a little song, read a good poem, see a fine picture, and if possible, speak a few reasonable words
                              Goethe

There are very few people on the planet that couldn't benefit from a good dose of awareness
                              Bill McEwen

The quickest way for one to understand the language of a species is to become a social partner

Konrad Lorenz

The hard stuff is moderately easy; the soft stuff is incredibly hard. Without the soft stuff, the hard stuff is meaningless

Meg Wheatley

Khe Sanh tested my soul; it didn't clean it. But Khe Sanh and the Viet Nam experience did offer me this as a basis of comparison: I survived thirteen months of war so I can certainly face my current challenge. There is only one reason that I escaped the experience unharmed: luck

Bill McEwen

When you've experienced a walk through the fire, there's nothing left to burn

Bill McEwen

When men found the mirror, they began to lose their soul

> *Unknown*

To be vulnerable takes an invulnerable core

> *Stephen Covey*

The enemy of the best is the good

> *Jim Collins*

The highest form of human motivation is to give trust

> *Stephen Covey*

The purpose of life is not to be happy. The purpose of life is to matter, have it make some difference that you lived at all

> *Leo Rostens*

Some pain in our lives is inevitable. However misery and suffering are always optional

> *Bill McEwen*

The deepest hunger of the human soul is to be understood

Stephen Covey

This is the main dilemma of our society: we are born, go to school, get jobs, get married, have children, grow old and die without ever knowing who we are

Unknown

A fool is someone who knows too much to learn anything

Noah Ben Shea ("Jacob the Baker")

The way to discover what is of value in life is by taking time to treasure the moments

Unknown

Better to have a diamond with a flaw than a polished pebble without

Bill Brown ("The American Field")

We know how to blow ourselves off the face of the earth but we don't begin to even understand what sexuality is all about

Scott Peck

Unless you walk out into the unknown, the odds of making a profound difference in your life are pretty slim

Tom Peters

In order to explore inner space, one has to be an explorer

Scott Peck

Because we live with the questions does not mean that we die with the answers. An open mind is the path to an open heart. When we have lost the way it is not the way that is lost

Noah Ben Shea ("Jacob the Baker")

We are not human beings on a spiritual journey; we are spiritual beings on a human journey

Stephen Covey

Only after the last tree has been cut down. Only after the last river has been poisoned. Only after the last fish has been caught. Only then will you find that money can't be eaten

A Cree Indian

The only way to pass any test is to take the test. It is inevitable

Black Swan

Be willing to be surprised by forces beyond your control and realize that a major learning on the journey is the art of surrender

Scott Peck

If today were my last, I have no regrets. It's not about what comes back; it's about what goes out. I had expressed my heart and that felt fantastic...I had stretched beyond fear and had gone out on the dance floor. I had put it on the line without demanding a guarantee of the results

Bill McEwen

I pretty well understand the concepts but have yet to live the reality

Bill McEwen (on Covey's 7 Habits)

You only live once but if you do it right once is enough

Ethiopian Proverb

Don't let ancient wisdom become a thing of the past

"The Qi Journal"

I clearly see that my life depends on what I decide to do with it. So much of life passes without our being in it at all

George Sheehan

It is good to have an end to journey towards, but it is the journey that matters, in the end

Ursula Le Guin

We must learn humility if we are to face the complexities we have created

Hazel Henderson

If some are still dominated by their former bad habits and can teach by their words, let them teach...for perhaps by being put to shame by their own words, they will begin to practice what they teach

Henri Nouween ("Reaching Out")

Forever is but a trail of "nows" and the best a man can do is to live each one fully in its turn

"The Horse Whisperer"

I understand that you help people who have horse problems. I help horses who have people problems. I'm not doing it for the people; I'm doing it for the horses. Eventually you will learn…it's the only difference between looking and seeing. Look long enough and if you're doing it right, you begin to see

"The Horse Whisperer"

When you're in transition with this material and really trying to apply and internalize, you never know where you'll come out

Chuck Farnsworth (On Covey's 7 Habits)

Freedom is just another word for nothing left to lose

Janis Joplin

Synchronicity- A meaningful coincidence of two or more events where something other than the probability of chance is involved

Joseph Jaworski ("Synchronicity")

In the middle of winter, I finally learned that there was in me an invincible summer

Camus

To coach (mentor) someone to be the best is a much higher honor than being the best

Dan Gable

People do not really know something until it falls from their heads to their hearts

Native American Concept of Knowledge

You never walk into a situation and believe that you know better than the natives

Unknown

The truth will set you free but first it will make you miserable

Paula Petty Ward

If we don't cry our tears, they store inside us and cause us harm...the crying is the healing and not the hurting. The hurting has already happened

Annette Goodheart

There are only two ways to live your life: one is though nothing is a miracle; the other is though everything is a miracle

Einstein

We could have flashed by one another like two pieces of cosmic dust...and we would have never known

"The Bridges of Madison County"

A good trainer can hear a horse speak to him. A great trainer can hear a horse whisper. You have to know the inside of a horse before you can capture the outside

"The Horse Whisperer"

Man's main concern is not to gain pleasure or to avoid pain but rather to find meaning in his life. That is why man is ever ready to suffer, on the condition to be sure, that his suffering has meaning

Viktor Frankl

The conclusion is always the same: love is still the most powerful and still the most unknown energy of the world

Teilhard de Chardin

It is only with the heart that one can see rightly; what is essential is invisible to the eye

Antoine De Saint-Exupery

With unfailing kindness, your life always presents what you need to learn. Whether you stay home or work in an office or whatever, the next teacher is going to pop right up

Charlotte Joko Beck

We are all children of the Great Spirit, and we all belong to Mother Earth. Our planet is in great trouble and if we keep carrying old grudges and do not work together, we will all die

Chief Seattle

A whole person is one who has both walked with God and wrestled with the devil

Carl Jung

When we come to the last moment of this lifetime and we look back across it, the only thing that's going to matter is what has been the quality of our love

Richard Bach

The only true yardstick by which the value of a course can be measured is the amount of inspiration, knowledge, and mental training which the students carry with them out of the classroom and into their lives

A.A. Kern

If you will open yourself to the natural environment, to the people around you, and to timeless principles and natural laws, you will find personal and specific answers to the challenges and opportunities which you face

The Sundance Promise

If we don't have the right perspective going in then we don't have a chance of finding that extraordinary view. When is the last time that you challenged your perceptions? There's always more than one right answer

DeWitt Jones

You can't learn anything from experiences that you're not having. If you want to be creative, go to where your questions lead you. There's a lot of seconds between birth and death when you're withdrawn from the game

Louis L 'Amour

Values control behavior; principles control consequences

Stephen Covey

Drop the ego, be real and watch what happens

"God on a Harley"

We must be willing to give up the life we've planned so as to have the life that's waiting for us

Joseph Campbell

A journey to the depths of the mind involve great personal risks, because we may not be able to endure what we find there

Karen Armstrong

Life at best is a changing, flowing process in which nothing is fixed. In my relationships with people, I have found that it does not help in the long run to act as though I am something that I am not. What is most personal is most general. Evaluation by others is not a guide for me. The facts are always friendly. I can trust my experience. Experience is for me the highest authority

Carl Rogers

Just because I teach this stuff doesn't mean that I live there all the time. I'm making my way through the chute just like everybody else

Chuck Farnsworth (On Covey's 7 Habits)

Your vision will become clear only when you look inside your heart. He who looks outside dreams; he who looks inside awakens

Carl Jung

A lot of the work which I've done has been based on the premise that addressing the underlying cause of a problem is ultimately more effective than addressing only its symptoms. We seem to be very adept at treating symptoms while ignoring root causes

Bill McEwen

Relationships always take time. Always

Unknown

I cannot teach people anything. I can only help them discover it within themselves

Bill McEwen

Whatever is flexible and flowing will tend to grow; whatever is rigid and blocked will die
Tao Te Ching

When you discover that you are riding a dead horse, the best strategy is to dismount
Dakota Indian

After thinking about it, I suppose that I'm a conservative revolutionary. I've embraced some revolutionary ideas but have done so in a very cautious, conservative, and robust fashion. I'm not throwing out all the old conventional models
Bill McEwen

When you label me, you negate me
Soren Kierkegaard

There is no coming to consciousness without some pain
Carl Jung

What you resist persists. Your truth will find you no matter where you hide

Unknown

The four agreements: be impeccable with your word; don't take anything personally; don't make assumptions; always do your best

("The Four Agreements")

I am an old man who has known a great many problems, most of which have never happened

Mark Twain

Surrender only signifies defeat in war; in life it signifies transcendence

Unknown

Love and death are our two greatest gifts. Unfortunately most of us pass them on unopened

Unknown

I have learned silence from the talkative, tolerance from the intolerant, and kindness from the unkind. Therefore, I should not be ungrateful to those teachers

Kahlil Gibran ("The Prophet")

When the bird and the book disagree, always believe the bird

John James Audubon

Nothing real can be threatened, nothing unreal exists. Herein rests the peace of God.

"A Course in Miracles"

If the eye is unobstructed, it results in sight. If the mind is unobstructed, wisdom arises

Unknown

Be present; Have fun; Choose my attitude; Make someone's day

("Fish")

Be with what is so that what is to be may become

Soren Kierkegaard

It is the refusal to heed that inner voice that causes the incurable sickness of the soul which makes us wither before our time

Unknown

The quality of our presence determines the quality of our life. Are we connected and present or are we disconnected and absent?

Jack Kornfield

Change your perspective, your viewpoint, or your location, and you will find your answer

Bill McEwen...from the Northwoods

A fool can ask questions that even a wise man can't answer

Ben Griffith...from the Northwoods

There is more to life than increasing its velocity

Gandhi

If every man and woman were to discover the meaning of their life and pursue it passionately, they would alter the social landscape overnight. In fact that's how lasting revolutions are made

Richard Bode

I was just thinking that of all the trails in this life that there is one that matters more than all the others. It is the trail of a true human being. I think you are on this trail, and it is good to see

From "Dances with Wolves"

The most important battle is the one you have with yourself. The only easy day was yesterday. Leadership by example is the way. Focus and never quit.

Bill McEwen (O.C.S. –Quantico- 1966)

Nothing is as good as it seems before we get it

Unknown

One sentence to live by: Be present in all your moments, live with integrity, respect the rights of others, and follow your heart

Unknown

Anything a human being can do I can do. In order to make peace with the shadow we must learn to live in the same house with the dragon

Carl Jung

A miracle is just a shift in perception. Our greatest tool for changing the world is our capacity to change our mind about the world. How a person seems to show up for us is intimately connected to how we show up for them. Infinite patience produces immediate results

Marianne Williamson ("Return to Love")

Simplicity is the whole secret of well being and traveling light brings with it a sense of intense energy and exhilaration. Between clinging and letting go, there always seems to be a struggle. No snowflake ever falls in the wrong place

("The Snow Leopard")

As you face a problem, remind yourself that you created it with one mind and you will solve it with another

Unknown

If a person is truly content with their belief system (their present one) no matter how destructive, leave them alone. I can't offer advice to anyone who's not ready to receive it. However, I can really begin to feel compassion when I think about what it might be like to live in their mind

Bill McEwen

The trees and stones will teach what you can never learn from the masters. Let the beauty we love be what we do

Rumi

Three of the most difficult things we do in life: return love for hate; including the excluded; apologizing (I was wrong!)

Unknown

Full attention is full acceptance is surrender

Eckhart Tolle ("The Power of Now")

I shall be telling this with a sigh somewhere ages and ages hence
Two roads diverged in a wood
And I...I took the one less traveled by and that has made all the difference

Robert Frost

Do you have the patience to wait till your mud settles and the water is clear?
Can you remain unmoving until the right action arises by itself?

Tao Te Ching

What you think of me is none of my business

Unknown

The everyday practice is simply to develop complete acceptance and openness to all situations, emotions, and people

Unknown

Pessimist- one who sees the brutal facts and quits
Optimist- one who has boundless faith and ignores the brutal facts
Realist- one who sees the brutal facts and has faith that they can be dealt with

The Stockdale Paradox

Turning points in life are sometimes misty, even murky places...you know the insight: now I realize what's important and will be forever changed

Bill McEwen

Private victory gives me the courage to make a contribution. Public victory allows me to make that contribution

Chuck Farnsworth

As long as we wish for safety we will have difficulty pursuing what matters

Peter Block

No matter where your obituary runs, a life well lived must mean that you sometimes HEAR the rabbit hit the ground with each bound

Walt Harrington

As I have learned, hunting is filled with pristine moments: the sound of a leaf falling through naked branches; the sound of that first gobble or of a flushing grouse...

Bill McEwen

Life is a banquet and the tragedy is that most people are starving to death. When there's something within you that moves in the right direction, it creates its own discipline. The day you teach the child the name of the bird, the child will never see the bird again...concepts only lead us to reality and when we get there we must each experience it for ourselves

Anthony De Mello ("Awareness")

If we were not making such an immense effort to separate ourselves from life, we might actually live day to day, minute by minute, as a series of predictable miracles

Joseph Jaworski ("Synchronicity")

The ultimate spiritual challenge is to wake up

Unknown

When mores are sufficient, laws are unnecessary. When mores are insufficient laws are unenforceable

Emile Durkheim

Always, we hope that someone else has the answer...that some other place will be better; some other time...it will all turn out. This is it. No one else has the answer; no other place will be better and it has already turned out. Search your heart

Unknown

When you get here to this moment of "now" each day becomes extraordinary. It is profound and ordinary at the same time

Eckhart Tolle ("The Power of Now")

Live your own life for you shall die your own death

Mike Gaddis ("Jenny Willow")

Nothing happens until something moves. Everything is just energy

Albert Einstein

Three principles of transformation: anything you resist, persists...and gets stronger; no two things can occupy the same space at the same time (fear/love); anything that you recreate or have be exactly as it is will complete itself and disappear (if you actually let things be the way they are, they disappear)

Unknown

When you lose touch with inner stillness, you lose touch with yourself. When you lose touch with yourself, you lose yourself in the world

Eckhart Tolle

Now this is the law of the jungle
As old and true as the sky
And the wolf that shall keep it may prosper
But the wolf that shall break it must die
As the creeper that girdles the tree trunk
The law runneth forward and back
For the strength of the pack is the wolf
And the strength of the wolf is the pack
Rudyard Kipling ("The Jungle Book")

The power of "we" is stronger than the power of "me"

Unknown

The reality of life is that your perceptions, right or wrong, influence everything you do. When you get a proper perspective of your perceptions, you may be surprised at how many other things fall into place

Roger Birkman

The mistreated body, mindful of its past neglect, eventually exacts repayment in full, with interest. Physical fitness can neither be acquired by wishful thinking or outright purchase. It must be earned one day at a time

Joseph Pilates

All endings are just beginnings. Sometimes we just don't know it

Mitch Albom ("Tuesdays with Morrie")

A clear conscious never fears midnight knocking

Chinese Proverb

I wouldn't give a fig for simplicity on this side of complexity. I would give my right arm for simplicity on the far side of complexity

Unknown

Because once it is accepted, the fact that life is difficult no longer matters

Scott Peck

If her past were your past, her pain your pain, her level of consciousness your level of consciousness, you would think and act exactly as she does. With this realization come compassion, forgiveness, and peace

Eckhart Tolle

If your life seems out of control, begin with the "5 minute" rule: spend 5 minutes today doing something that will make tomorrow better

Roger Merrill

There are moments in your life when you must act, even though you cannot carry your best friends with you. The "still small voice" within you must always be the final arbiter when there is a conflict of duty

Gandhi

We are always in the world. It's HOW we're in the world that matters

Cynthia Keen

The gap between what I want verses what I need/know is the space in which private victory is fought

Bill McEwen

I am attempting to live MINDFULLY in a world of change and impermanence. By slowing down and by changing the way I look at things, amazingly, the things I look at begin to change

Bill McEwen

Most ailing organizations have developed a functional blindness to their own defects. They are not suffering because they cannot resolve their problems but because they cannot see their problems

John Gardner

Timeless Wisdom for Challenging Times

The real challenge as 3,000 years of wisdom reminds us lies in simple everyday living. Without slowness and mindfulness, there's only more chatter. I have allowed the great blue heron, standing motionless on one leg, to teach me the art of patience. I have also been privileged to learn awareness and patience from a 4 year old gobbler. All the lessons abound if we would only pay attention

Bill McEwen

We are knee deep in a river searching for water

Unknown

If you want to make minor incremental changes and improvements, work on practices, behavior, and attitude. But if you want to make significant quantum improvement over the long haul, work on paradigms and perceptions

Stephen Covey

Tell him what you want him to do; show him how to do it; then make him do it; read the dog and know how to read the sheep

Ivan Bowen on Dog Training

This is my simple religion. There is no need for temples; no need for complicated philosophy. Our own brain our own heart is our temple. The philosophy is kindness

The Dali Lama

The quality of your plan is not as important as the quality of your execution

Unknown

I have learned that when I allow and accept what is life, flows much smoother, and I experience inner peace. Also, I have learned that when I become defensive about something, I have identified with an illusion

Bill McEwen

I've got the time I've got and what I do takes the time it takes

> *Melissa Walker ("Wilderness Time")*

I am convinced that in the final analysis there is no situation which does not contain the seed of meaning

> *Viktor Frankl*

Three organizational myths: those who have been there the longest know the most; those who have the highest positions are the smartest; everything that I'm working on is important

> *Harry Brittan*

If you know and really understand the laws of nature and obey them, then nature will treat you kindly

> *Bill McEwen*

Lasting change happens when people see for themselves that a different way of life is more fulfilling than their present one

Unknown

Why can't you see? Freedom is sometimes just simply another perspective away. If your lens was changed for a moment, who could you be?

Colton Watson...7 Habits Student

Life is a one way street. No matter how many detours you take, none of them lead back. Once you know and accept this, life becomes much simpler

Unknown

Communication is very hard when dealing with an unconscious person

Bill McEwen

If you live each day as if it were your last, someday you'll most certainly be right. Life is nothing but a series of moments. Start living the moments, and the years will take care of themselves

Unknown

The important things in life never happen by accident. But even with those things that were meant to be, sometimes we have to wait awhile and then maybe give them a little nudge

Nicholas Evans ("The Smoke Jumper")

No man can earn his heart's desire
Lest first he braves the smoke and the fire

Nicholas Evans ("The Smoke Jumper")

To me the fundamental problem is that we have confused rules with principles. Rules can be bent but principles cannot

James Owen ("Cowboy Ethics")

Many events in our lives are designed to get our attention in order that we might correct our course. If we continue to focus on the event, we may miss the clue inside the event which could be an important life changing lesson. Our challenge is to absorb the lesson and throw away the experience

Bill McEwen

Live each day with courage; take pride in your work; always finish what you start; do what has to be done; be tough, but fair; when you make a promise, keep it; talk less and say more; know where to draw the line; remember that some things are not for sale; ride for the brand

James Owen ("Cowboy Ethics")

Thank you for sharing the dance. The powerful play goes on and you may contribute a verse

Walt Whitman

The ultimate trick to life is not to be in the know but to be in the mystery

Unknown

Awakening is a shift in consciousness in which thinking and awareness separate. Awareness is a conscious connection with universal intelligence. Another word for it is presence: consciousness without thought. Our inner purpose is to WAKE UP

Eckhart Tolle

If all the beasts were gone, man would die from loneliness of spirit. For whatever happens to the beasts, happens to man. All things are connected. Whatever befalls the earth, befalls the sons of the earth

Chief Seattle

We can all be heroes in our own lives

Unknown

The value of a human being, to a large extent, is determined by the degree to which he or she is free of self

Albert Einstein

The root cause of all human suffering is one simple yet profoundly tragic mistake: the ignorance of our true nature

From "Diamond in Your Pocket"

There is a difference between pain and suffering: pain is a sensation in the body at a particular time. Suffering is spread out over time and must be accompanied by some story about the pain. We all will have some pain in our lives; however, misery and suffering are optional

Bill McEwen

The morning breeze has secrets to tell you. Do not go back to sleep

Rumi

The persistent and constant pressure of gravity on misaligned bodies is the primary reason for many physical ailments

Randy Mack...Certified Rolfer

Good wine makes daily living easier, less hurried with fewer tensions and more tolerance

Benjamin Franklin

From where the sun now stands, I will fight no more forever

Chief Joseph, October 1877

Anything that can be asserted without evidence can also be dismissed without evidence

Christopher Hitchens

I am condemned to a life of making choices

Bill McEwen

Getting fit is no different than navigating a failing company back to health. Analyze, execute a plan, then track and monitor results. It really comes down to what you commit to, and in the long run it's all about self-discipline

Bill McEwen

Lameness is an impediment to the leg, not to the will. If you stick around cripples long enough, mental or physical, pretty soon you'll learn how to limp

From "Stoic Warriors"

If you pursue things not in your power, you will be hindered, you will lament, you will be disturbed, and you will blame both Gods and men

Epictetus

Consciousness without thought...how am I doing?

Bill McEwen

The Rolfing process is about relationships. Not everything that is faced can be changed. But nothing can be changed until it is faced. All living bodies are energy systems which strive to maintain themselves in a state of equilibrium

"The Rolf Line"

All my patients get healed. They don't all get well. My antagonist is my friend. Start the breathing and you start the healing

J. Michael Wood...Qi Gong Instructor

Today we are faced with the pre-eminent fact that if civilization is to survive, we must cultivate the science of human relationships

Franklin D. Roosevelt

I am a deeply religious non-believer. This is a new kind of religion

Albert Einstein

Six emotional cancers: complaining, comparing, criticizing, competing, contending, and complacency

Stephen Covey

I've reached an age when if someone tells me I have to wear socks, I really don't have to. And I have found out that if I don't care what other people think, I can be comfortable most anywhere

Bill McEwen

The Americans have the watches, but we have the time. We might not come back in a week or a year, but you can bet your britches that we'll come back

The Taliban

To meet everything and everyone in stillness instead of mental noise is the greatest gift that you can offer the universe

Eckhart Tolle

We all have baggage. The question is what baggage are you willing to deal with? Three key questions:

1. *Is this a problem that you want to work on? Are you ready to release it?*
2. *Are you willing to learn what you need to know to get well?*
3. *Are you willing to let me teach you what you need to know?*

J. Michael Wood...Qi Gong Instructor

It'll get you there before you know you're on the bus

Bill McEwen on "Gentleman Jack"

Telling your story is the beginning of healing

Carl Jung

You believe that work tires you? Work can never tire you. What tires you are your worries about the past and your anxiety about the future

"The Fall of the Human Intellect"

I have a bit of advice to offer. Hold on to the people you are close to and love them fiercely. Get up every morning and live like there's no tomorrow...because one day you'll find it's true

Chuck P. Farrer

It is how we feel about an experience that determines that determines how we feel about an experience

Michael Brown

The defining challenge of the 21st century will be to face the reality that humanity shares a common fate on a crowded planet

Unknown

The only thing consistent about ruffed grouse hunting is inconsistency

Ben Griffith...The Northwoods, 2008

What is a life well lived? I think it has to do with contentment and living every moment/day with mindfulness and gratitude

Bill McEwen

Having to squeeze the last drop of utility out of the land has the same desperate finality as having to chop up the furniture to keep warm

Aldo Leopold

Those who would preserve the spirit must also look after the body to which it is attached

Albert Einstein

When you tell me I forget. When you show me I remember. When you involve me I understand

Chinese Proverb

If we pick up anyone and carry them, when the time comes to put them down, their feet will land in exactly the same spot from which we picked them up

Unknown

We cannot change the cause of anything by fiddling with its effect. We're very good at treating symptoms and ignoring root causes

Michael Brown

Conservation is a state of harmony between nature and man

Aldo Leopold

When the heart is allowed to work its alchemy, we discover that we can transmute our pain into peace, our grief into joy, and our anger into serenity

Michael Brown

Men think in herds; it will be seen that they go mad in herds while they only recover their senses slowly and one by one

Charles McKay

The first step in wellness is being a part of your health, in taking responsibility

Unknown

My spirituality is in my conscious and consistent response to my heart

Bill McEwen

If we could see the wisdom in a single flower, our whole world would change

Unknown

Why put things off until tomorrow, because tomorrow will also be a busy day

Unknown

The way we breathe is an exact reflection of the way we're living our life. Are we connected and present or are we disconnected and absent?

Michael Brown

Nothing is to be clung to as I, me, or mine

Buddhist Teaching

When we remain intimately obedient to what represents our personal ethics, crashing is highly unlikely

Michael Brown

Growth is the process of changing, or at least carefully examining, your perceptions

Stephen Covey

The most important question that people have asked throughout history is "what is my life's purpose"?

Norman Shealy

Bill's turkey hunting guidelines...in order of importance:

1. *Position...set up, sitting position, gun placement etc.*
2. *Perspective...think like a turkey, be present/aware, know the woods*
3. *Patience...nature never gets in a hurry, so why should we? When you THINK that you're ready to move, wait another thirty minutes. This will kill more turkeys than any call on the market*
4. *Passion and Persistence...you must love it and hang tough. Fourteen days in a row is brutal*
5. *Calling...much overrated; duplicate only what you hear in the woods*

Bill McEwen

Knowing how to listen requires patience and compassion. You do not listen in order to judge, criticize, or evaluate. You listen for one reason alone: to allow the other to express himself/herself. The practice of deep listening consists of keeping compassion alive in your heart the whole time you are listening

Unknown

The purpose of my teaching/facilitation is simply this: to create a heightened sense of awareness/consciousness in individuals and organizations so that they begin to focus on root causes and not just focus on their symptoms

Bill McEwen

Time only matters when you're catching a plane or sitting in jail

Unknown

A clouded mirror cannot reflect accurately. Without clarity in our relationship to ourselves, we will have a hard time improving our relationship with others

Bill McEwen

The vital function that pets fulfill in this world hasn't been fully recognized. They keep millions of people sane

Eckhart Tolle

Everything natural, every flower, tree, and animal has important lessons to teach us if we would only STOP, LOOK, and LISTEN

Eckhart Tolle

If I have been able to see further, it was only because I stood on the shoulders of giants

Sir Isaac Newton

The oldest task in human history is to live on a piece of land without spoiling it

Aldo Leopold

On twenty three years of ruffed grouse hunting in Wisconsin: Blue Sky; Bright Leaves; The Smell of Fall; Frost; Quaking Aspens; Golden Tamaracks; Ripe Thorn Apples; The Northwoods; Solitude; Soaring Eagles; A Flushing Grouse; A Man; His Dogs; Life Simple; Life Complete

Bill McEwen

It's the mark of an educated mind to be able to entertain a thought without accepting it

Aristotle

How much of your life do you spend looking forward to being somewhere else?

Bill McEwen

Close your eyes and ask: Who am I? What do I want? What is my purpose? Watch your breath for five minutes. We don't have to have all the answers. Live the questions and life will move you into the answers

Unknown

There's no short term fix for a chronic long term problem

Ray Lahood

I am letting go is a powerful practice

Bill McEwen

This mind and body is our household. If this inner household is not in order, no outer household can be in order

Ayya Khema

There's a thread you follow. It goes among things that change. But it doesn't change. People wonder about what you are pursuing. You have to explain about the thread. But it's hard for others to see. While you hold it you can't get lost. Tragedies happen; people get hurt or die; and you suffer and get old. Nothing you do can stop time's unfolding. You don't ever let go of the thread.

William Stafford ("The Way It Is")

The purpose of all major religious traditions is not to construct big temples on the outside, but to create temples of goodness on the INSIDE

The Dali Lama

The essential truth of suffering is that neither individual nor social problems are due to external conditions

B. Alan Wallace

Coming to our senses is the work of no time at all, only of being present and awake in the here and now. It is also paradoxically, a lifetime's engagement

Jon Kabat-Zin

Almost everything is ultimately out of our control, and I think that we're really waking up to that

Jim Collins

You can expect certain benefits from meditation. The initial ones are the practical things; the later stages are profoundly transcendental. They run together from the simple to the sublime

Bante Henepola Gunaratana

If the desire to write is not accompanied by actual writing then the desire is not to write

Hugh Prather

Enlightenment: that magnificent escape from anguish and ignorance- never happens by accident. It results from the brave and sometimes lonely battle of one person against his own weaknesses

Bikkhu Nyanasobhano

When someone asks you a question, answer him or her sincerely, and when you are not asked, do not force your teaching upon others

Jae Woong Kim

Fear is static that prevents me from hearing my intuition

Hugh Prather

Sometimes the best we can do may be very good, sometimes it is only mediocre

Ayya Khema

If we do not try, we will not know

Ayya Khema

It is often thought that the Buddha's doctrine teaches us that suffering will disappear if one has mediated long enough, or if one sees everything differently. Suffering isn't going to go away; the one who suffers is going to go away

Ayya Khema

Where there is confusion is where peace can arise. When confusion is penetrated with understanding, what remains is peace

Ajahn Chah

Everything is as it is. It has no name other than the name we give it. It is we who call it something; we give it a value. We say this thing is good or it's bad, but in itself, the thing is only as it is. It's not absolute, it's just as it is. People are just as they are

Ajahn Sumedho

I do my thing and you do your thing. I am not in this world to live up to your expectations, and you are not in this world to live up to mine. You are you and I am I, and if by chance we find each other, it's beautiful. If not, it can't be helped

Fritz Perls ("Gestalt Prayer")

The true value of a human being is determined primarily by the measure and the sense in which he has attained liberation from the self

Albert Einstein

Fill your bowl to the brim, and it will spill. Keep sharpening your knife and it will blunt. Chase after money and security, and your heart will never unclench. Care about people's approval, and you will be their prisoner. DO YOUR WORK, THEN STEP BACK. THE ONLY PATH TO SERENITY

Stephen Mitchell ("Tao Te Ching")

The Buddha stated clearly that saying only what is true is not sufficient for skillful speech. Speaking skillfully also requires saying what is useful for the listener to hear

Rodney Smith

If I were to sum up the last forty years of my life, the time since I became a monk, I would have to say that it has been an ongoing lesson in the extent of my own stupidity

Soko Morinaga

We always imagine that there's got to be somewhere else better than where we are right now; this is the great SOMEWHERE ELSE we all carry around in our heads. We believe SOMEWHERE ELSE is out there for us if we could only find it. But there's no SOMEWHERE ELSE. Everything is right here
Brad Warner

Keep it simple; stick to the present moment
Ajahn Chah

I went to the woods because I wished to live deliberately, to front only the essential facts of life and see if I could not learn what it had to teach and not, when I came to die, discover that I had not lived
Henry David Thoreau

A good teacher wants nothing more than to see you stand on your own two feet
Ezra Bayda and Josh Bartok

If you move into pure awareness in the midst of pain, even for the tiniest moment, your relationship with the pain is going to shift right in that very moment. It is impossible for it not to change because the gesture of holding it, even if not sustained for long, even for a second or two, already reveals its larger dimensionality

Jon Kabat-Zin

No matter how hard you try to free yourself, until you see the value of freedom and the pain of bondage, you won't be able to let go

Ajahn Chah

Doubt-in everything- is absolutely essential. Everything, no matter how great, how fundamental, how beautiful or important it is, must be questioned

Brad Warner

If we are serious in our desire for a judicial system that heals, we must find a way to divert our focus from punishing guilt to transforming intention

David R. Loy

In what I'm doing, I can only focus on making a difference in one life at a time

Bill McEwen

If you respect the Northwoods they will treat you kindly; if you disrespect the Northwoods and get careless, they are unforgiving

Bill McEwen (on 23 years experience)

The basic paradox: everything is a mess yet all is well

Ezra Bayda and Josh Bartok

A man with no soul will always be a poor man, one way or another

Elmer Kelton

We are sure to die. This is so true it scarcely bears mentioning, it seems. But it is also true through the momentum of desire and action we find ourselves always assuming, taking for granted, another gracious stretch of days to wander through- year upon forgiving year in which we may leisurely revise our philosophies, start or close agreeable projects, and maybe settle someday into some kind of religious faith. Unmindful of death, we grow negligent and live like the froth on a splashing stream- disoriented, weightless, and without conviction

Bikkhu Nyanasobhano

In the pursuit of learning, every day something is acquired. In the pursuit of Tao, every day something is dropped

Lao Tzu ("Tao Te Ching")

Qi Gong can reveal the mystery of life. It is the best way to further world medical science and bring health, longevity, and wisdom to humankind

Tzu Kuo Shih

The more I doubted the more I meditated, the more I practiced. Whenever doubt arose, I practiced right at that point. Wisdom arose. Things began to change. It's hard to describe the change that took place. The mind changed until there was no more doubt. I don't know how it changed. If I were to try telling someone, they probably wouldn't understand

Ajahn Chah

When you visit someone in the hospital, talk to the person, and leave the doctors and nurses to talk to the sickness

Ajahn Brahm

If you do external exercises, you must do internal exercises

Taoist Proverb

The occurrence of disease is due to insufficiently balanced Qi

Nei Ching

Life is a good teacher and a good friend. Things are always in transition, if we could only realize it. Nothing ever sums itself up in the way we like to dream about. This very moment is the perfect teacher, and, lucky for us, it is with us wherever we are

Pema Chodron

You already have the precious mixture that will make you well. Use it

Rumi

Change the world, change your mind, change yourself. It's all connected

Kate Wheeler

Qi Gong training is a way to conserve our essence, balance our energy, and raise up our spirit

Stanley Wilson

For breath is life, and if you breathe well you will live long on earth

Sanskrit Proverb

The men of old breathed clear down to their heals

Chuang Tzu

Wisdom is a way of knowing that goes beyond one's mind and rational understanding and embraces the whole person: mind, body, heart, and soul

Unknown

When all is said and done, the only change that will make a difference is the transformation of the human heart

Joe Jaworski

How much longer will I live? Only one thing seems very clear to me: every day, every moment should be well lived. What a simple truth! Still it is worth my attention. Did I bring a smile to someone's face? Did I feel gratitude for my blessings? Did I let go of anger, resentments? Did I love?

Bill McEwen

Virtually all indigenous or native cultures have regarded nature or universe or Mother Earth as the ultimate teacher. At few times in history has there been a greater need to rediscover this teacher

Peter Senge (From "Presence")

The biggest surprise on the soulful journey to authenticity, whether as a philosophy or a spiritual path, is that the path is a spiral. We go up but we go in circles. Each time around the view gets a little bit wider

Sarah Breathnach

Where there is surrender, synchronicity tends to follow

Unknown

When people who are actually creating a system start to see themselves as the source of their problems, they invariably discover a new capacity to create the results they truly desire

Peter Senge ("Presence")

Operating from a larger intention brings into play forces one could never tap from just trying to impose our will on a situation

Joe Jaworski

What does it mean to act in the world and not on the world?

C. Otto Scharmer

Aging, illness, and death are treasures for those who understand them. They're Noble Truths, Noble Treasures. If they were people, I'd bow down to them every day

Ajaan Lee

Our life isn't divided up into practice and nonpractice caring for the body and caring for the mind. It is one seamless web, and awareness is the key

J. Krishnamurti

No matter which spiritual path you pursue the nuts and bolts of transformation wind up looking pretty much the same: surrender, compassion, detachment, forgiveness. We all have to go through the same eye of the needle to get where our true heart lies

Sarah Breathnach

All that we are attached to is impermanent- so there's nothing to get ruffled about

Sara L. Weber

Overcoming attachment does not mean becoming cold and indifferent. On the contrary it means learning to have relaxed control over our mind through a good understanding of the real causes of happiness and fulfillment. This enables us to enjoy life more and suffer less

Kathleen McDonald

If you want to untie a knot, you must look at the cord carefully and then gently undo the tangle. Yanking at the cord will only make the knot tighter

Thomas Hanna

The body should be supple like an infant; the movements should be flexible like a snake; the feeling should be soft like water; the breathing should be smooth like a cloud

Qi Gong Proverb

People usually fail when they are on the verge of success. So give as much care to the end as to the beginning. Then there will be no failure

Lao Tzu ("Tao Te Ching")

No, wilderness is not a luxury but a necessity of the human spirit, and as vital to our lives as water and good bread. A civilization which destroys what is left of the wild, the spare, the original, is cutting itself off from its origins and betraying the principle of civilization itself

Edward Abbey ("Desert Solitaire")

Every GOOD hunter is uneasy in the depths of his conscious when faced with the death he is about to inflict on the enchanting animal

Jose Ortega y Gasset ("Meditations on Hunting")

Why have I made the trip to the shores of Lake Superior and the Northwoods for the last twenty three Octobers? Quite simply, I continue to go back for the PURITY of the experience and to continue to learn. The great teacher is the wilderness: the vastness of the forests, the unpredictability of the weather, the many species of wildlife including eagles, black bears, and wolves. Finally, one of the last PURE upland bird hunting experiences is in the pursuit of the ruffed grouse

Bill McEwen

There are three truths- traditionally called the three marks- of our existence: suffering, impermanence, and egolessness

Pema Chodron

Fear is the main ingredient of pain. It's what makes pain HURT. Take away the fear and only feeling itself is left

Ajahn Brahm

In our practice...it is not what we do, it is HOW we do. It is not what we think, it is HOW we think, not what we feel but HOW we feel. This is a very important aspect of our teaching. In this way we learn to take full responsibility for ourselves. We can never blame another for our actions or reactions

Cherri Huber

...To sum up, one does not hunt in order to kill; on the contrary, one kills in order to have hunted. If one were to present the sportsman with the death of the animal as a gift, he would refuse it. What he is after is having to win it to conquer it through his own effort and skill with all the extras this carries with it: the immersion in the countryside, the healthfulness of the exercise, the distraction from his job, and so on and so forth

Jose Ortega y Gasset ("Meditations on Hunting")

Who would you be without your story?

Byron Katie

When walking or resting in nature, honor that realm by being there fully. Be still. Be aware. The contemplation of nature can free you of that "ME", the big troublemaker

Eckhart Tolle

Hunting for me is not about the taking of the game but being at one with nature, the woods, the sights, sounds, and smells

Bill McEwen

What business have I in the woods, if I am thinking of something out of the woods?

Henry David Thoreau

Remaining ignorant is a full time job. The truth is always here. We have to work hard not to see it

Cheri Huber

During a trip to the wilds, it often takes individuals a week or more to forget the frenetic lives they have led, but inevitably the feeling of timelessness does come, often without warning...I know now as individuals accept the time clock of the wilderness, their lives become entirely different. It is one of the great compensations of primitive experience, and when one finally reaches the point where days are governed by daylight and dark, rather than by schedules, where one eats when hungry and sleeps when tired, and becomes completely immersed in the ancient rhythms, then one begins to live

Sigurd F. Olson

There's a trade-off between what we do today and the impact of today's decisions on future generations

Peter Senge

Do you need more knowledge? Is more information going to save the world, or faster computers, more scientific or intellectual analysis? Is it not wisdom that humanity needs most at this time? But what is wisdom and where is it to be found? Wisdom comes with the ability to be still. Just look and listen. No more is needed. Being still, looking and listening activate the non-conceptual intelligence within you. Let stillness direct your words and actions. True intelligence operates silently

Eckhart Tolle

Things that matter most must never be at the mercy of things which matter least

Johann Goethe

All things are created twice. First is the mental creation, intention, or plan; second is the physical creation, action, or work. Highly effective people clearly see the outcome they want in every area of life before they act

  Stephen Covey (From the "7 Habits")

The following was found on a bottle of Schlafly's Pumpkin Ale given to me by my nephew, John, on November 15, 2011: "I would rather sit on a pumpkin and have it all to myself than be crowded on a velvet cushion"

  Henry David Thoreau

If we study but don't practice, we won't get results. It's like a man who raises chickens but doesn't collect the eggs. All he gets is chicken shit! To get the best results you must study and practice as well

  Ajahn Chah

The next step in human evolution is to transcend thought. This is now our urgent task. It doesn't mean not to think anymore, but simply not to be completely identified with thought, possessed by thought

Eckhart Tolle

There was something formless and perfect before the universe was born. It is serene. Empty. Solitary. Unchanging. Infinite. Eternally present. It is the mother of the universe. For lack of a better name, I call it the Tao

Lao Tzu ("Tao Te Ching")

Enough. These few words are enough. If not these words, this breath. If not this breath, just this sitting here. This opening to the life we have refused... again and again... until now. UNTIL NOW

David Whyte

We are such spendthrifts with our lives...I'm not running for sainthood. I just happen to think that in life we need to be a little like the farmer who puts back into the soil what he takes out

Paul Newman

The juice goes out of Christianity when it becomes too based on faith rather than living like Jesus or seeing the world as Jesus saw it. I think different religions are different doors to the same house. Sometimes I think the house exists, sometimes I think it doesn't. It's the great mystery

Steve Jobs

When asked where she lived, one of my friends, who is also one of my neighbors, replied: "I live between nowhere and the far side of somewhere"

"Barbee" Heilman

Get current. Make sure you're not still carrying around old ideas about yourself that aren't really applicable to your present life...and perhaps never were

Cherie Huber

To become your own psychologist, you don't have to learn some big philosophy. All you have to do is to examine your own mind every day. You already examine material things every day...every morning you check out the food in your kitchen...but you never investigate your mind. Checking your mind is much more important

Lama Yeshe

If I knew all there is to know about a golden arctic poppy growing on a rocky ledge in the Far North, I would know the whole story of evolution and creation

Sigurd Olson

In 1979 I decided to become a nun. Up until that time, I had tried a lot of things and had seen that the world cannot make one happy. In the course of these travels it became clear to me that tranquility and peace have nothing to do with the most beautiful places on earth or the most interesting experiences. They are only to be found in the human heart

Ayya Khema

Consider the lilies of the field, how they grow; they toil not, neither do they spin: And yet I say unto you, that even Solomon in all his glory was not arrayed like one of these

The Bible (Mathew 6:28, 29)

We wonder how people can't see the most obvious things about themselves...yet we forget those people are us

Ezra Bayda with Josh Bartok

Notice how PRESENT a flower is, how surrendered to life...you need nature as your teacher to help you reconnect with Being. But not only do you need nature, it also needs you... A great silent space holds all of nature in its embrace. It also holds you...only when your noisy mind subsides can you connect with nature at a deep level

Eckhart Tolle

One can live with people traveling the wilds in primitive ways, but not with aircraft, outboards, ATV's, or snowmobiles, no matter how muted they may be. Silence is one of the most important parts of a wilderness experience; without it the land is nothing more than rocks, trees, and water

Sigurd Olson

There are no shortcuts to anything worthwhile

Bill McEwen

Meditation is the only intentional and systematic activity which at bottom is about NOT trying to improve yourself or get anywhere else, but simply to realize where you already are. Perhaps its value lies precisely in this. Maybe we all need to do one thing in our lives simply for its own sake

Jon Kabat-Zinn

This is the gospel of Rolfing: when the body gets working appropriately, the force of gravity can flow through. Then the body heals itself, spontaneously

Ida Rolf

Energy can neither be created nor destroyed; it only changes form

Albert Einstein

When you can truly see the other person's viewpoint, you can forgive from the heart

Susan Reeve and Sherri Rosenthal

The body operates on energy, with energy, by energy: creating its own energy and taking in outside energy. A body is an individual energy machine...if you have a liver structure that is functioning very badly and the rest of your body is doing very well, you will be taking away energy store to keep that liver going...this is the important concept: that Rolfers are INTEGRATING something; we are not RESTORING something

Ida Rolf

Regardless of the form or philosophical basis, all Qi Gongs have this much in common. They all require that the practitioner learns to regulate and focus on breath, posture (body) and intent (mind)

Bill McEwen

Everything is mind made

Ayya Khema

Life begins with our first breath and will end after our last. To contemplate breathing is to contemplate life itself...the act of breathing begins our life as we come out of the womb; in our last moment, when we cease breathing, our life is over. It only makes sense that the breath should also have a profound influence on all the moments in between

Larry Rosenberg

Several years ago, I had a real revelation: because my breath was so unassuming, I had been completely undervaluing it...now I understand that it is the key to unlocking many doors and balancing mind, body, heart, and soul

Bill McEwen

Breathing in, I know that I am breathing in. Breathing out, I know that I'm breathing out

Thich Nhat Hanh

A good definition of Qi Gong: effort over a period of time put into the practice of working with the energy of life for the purpose of being able to sense, acquire, store, and mobilize Qi (Energy) at will in order to promote health, vitality, and longevity at will

"Qi" (Journal of Traditional Eastern Health)

It is not the philosopher's job in life to make things difficult, but difficult things simple. So here is the simple truth. The greatest challenge in life is daring to be who we are

Noah benShea

When you contemplate the big, and full sunrise, the more mindful and concentrated you are, the more the beauty of the sunrise revealed to you

Thich Nhat Hanh

The most powerful technique I know to protect your health is absolutely free...and literally right under your nose. If I had to limit all my advice on leading a healthy lifestyle to just one tip, it would be simply to learn how to breathe correctly. From my own experience and from working with patients, I have come to believe that proper breathing in the master key to good health

Dr. Andrew Weil

The ultimate promise of mindfulness...is that it helps us understand that our conventional view of ourselves and even that of what we mean by "self" is incomplete in some very important ways. Mindfulness helps us recognize how and why we mis-take the actuality of things for some story we create, and then makes it possible to chart a path toward greater sanity, well- being, and purpose

Jon Kabat-Zinn

Over the years I've learned one of the great laws of life: when I stop resisting a tense situation, my "shaky" energy calms down

Bill McEwen

Buddhist teachings are not a religion, they are a science of the mind

The Dali Lama

In popular Western culture we are taught that the way to achieve happiness is to change our external environment to fit our wishes. But this strategy doesn't work. In every life, pleasure and pain, gain and loss, praise and blame keep showing up, no matter how hard we struggle to have only pleasure, gain, and praise. Buddhist psychology offers a different approach to happiness, teaching that states of consciousness are far more crucial than outer circumstances

Jack Kornfield

There is no need to struggle to be free; the absence of struggle itself is freedom

Chogyam Trungpa

Ask yourself, and yourself alone, one question. Does this path have a heart? All paths are the same; they lead nowhere. There are paths going through the bush or into the brush...Does this path have a heart? If it does, the path is good; if it doesn't it is of no use

Don Juan (Carlos Castaneda)

Our ideas of a separate self are created by identification. The less we cling to ideas of self, the freer and happy we will be

Jack Kornfield

Thoughts are often one-sided and untrue. Learn to be mindful of thought instead of being lost in it

Jack Kornfield

After more than a century of looking for it, brain researchers have long since concluded that there is no conceivable place for a self to be located in the physical brain and that it simply does not exist

"Time Magazine", 2002

One of the first things I like to do each morning is meditate. I allocate 15 minutes, or more if I can; I'll just sit and focus my attention on my breathing, body sensations...all the while being a "casual observer" of my thoughts. I find that this peaceful ritual helps me start the day with a clear mind and a relaxed body

Bill McEwen

We come to think there is a method, a rational way to get from here to there, all the while confirming a view that where we are is somehow wrong or insufficient

Barry Magid

When one is willing to see all conflicts-whether physical, emotional, or mental- as dances of energy, and to accept them and to blend with them, options and opportunities for successful resolution emerge, powerfully and elegantly

Tom Crum

My friends it is through the establishment of the lovely clarity of mindfulness that you can let go of grasping after past and future, overcome attachment and grief, abandon all clinging and anxiety, and awaken an unshakable freedom of heart, here, now

The Buddha

Nature goes her own way, and all that to us seems an exception is really according to order

Goethe

Change does not take time, it takes commitment

Tom Crum

There is Suffering. There is the Cause of Suffering. There is the End of Suffering. There is the Path to the End of Suffering. These Four Noble Truths teach suffering and the end of suffering

The Buddha

He who bind himself to a joy
Doeth the winged life destroy
He who kisses the joy as it flies
Lives in eternity's sunrise

William Blake

Simple things done over an extended period of time have the most profound effect. One minute of focused concentration per day results in an hour of concentration in two months

Ayya Khema

Words cannot explain reality; only direct experience enables us to see the true face of reality. This teaching is merely a vehicle to describe the truth. It's like a raft that carries you to the other shore. The raft is needed but it's not the other shore. The finger is needed to know where to look for the moon but if you mistake the finger for the moon itself, you will never know the real moon

Ajahn Chah

Concentration is the secret of strength. You can't chase two rabbit's at once

Bill McEwen

If you want to say anything that could be hurtful and is untrue, don't say it; helpful and untrue, don't say it; hurtful and true, don't say it; helpful and true, find the right time

The Buddha

My mind is like a restless monkey: continually chattering and jumping from limb to limb

Bill McEwen

Today was a great day: I planted a pink dogwood and a Norway spruce. Everyone should try to plant at least one tree in their lifetime

Bill McEwen (Thanksgiving 2011)

The native peoples of America spoke of true stewardship of the earth which required keeping in mind the future of those at least seven generations beyond ours. We would do well to tend the world in such a way. After all, those unborn generations...ARE US

Bill McEwen

I think that my purpose in life is to live in harmony with and to maintain a CONSCIOUS connection with natural laws and universal intelligence.
Everything else is just background music!

Bill McEwen

Some Books which have impacted my life...
In no particular order

1. *"Tao Te Ching" - Stephen Mitchell*
2. *"The Power of Now" - Eckhart Tolle*
3. *"The 7 Habits of Highly Effective People" - Stephen R. Covey*
4. *"Man's Search for Meaning" - Viktor Frankl*
5. *"The Bible"*
6. *"The Presence Process"- Michael Brown*
7. *"Food for the Heart" - Ajahn Chah*
8. *"Coming to Our Senses" and "Full Catastrophe Living" - Jon Kabat-Zinn*
9. *"Ida Rolf Talks About Rolfing and Physical Reality" - Rosemary Feitis*
10. *"The Essential Aldo Leopold" - edited by Curt Meine and Richard Knight*
11. *"Best Way to Train Your Gun Dog" - Delmar Smith*
12. *"Leadership and the New Science" - Margaret J. Wheatley*
13. *"A New Earth" - Eckhart Tolle*

14. *"Jenny Willow" - Mike Gaddis*
15. *"Synchronicity...The Inner Path to Leadership" - Joseph Jaworski*
16. *"Tuesday's With Morrie" - Mitch Albom*
17. *"Chasing Daylight" - Eugene O'Kelly*
18. *"Meditations on Hunting" - Jose Ortega Y Gasset*
19. *"Breath by Breath...The Liberating Practice of Insight Meditation" - Larry Rosenberg*
20. *"When Things Fall Apart...Heart Advice for Difficult Times" - Pema Chodron*
21. *"Reflections From the North Country" - Sigurd Olson*
22. *"Stillness Speaks" - Eckhart Tolle*
23. *"Being Nobody, Going Nowhere" - Ayya Khema*
24. *"Chinese Medical Qi Gong Therapy" - Jerry Alan Johnson*
25. *"Awareness" - Anthony De Mello*

26. *"The Tao of Natural Breathing" - Dennis Lewis*
27. *"Zen in the Art of Archery" - Eugene Herrigel*
28. *"The Heart of the Buddha's Teaching" - Thich Nhat Hanh*
29. *"I and Thou" - Martin Buber*
30. *"Conscious Breathing" - Gay Hendricks*

Acknowledgements

So many people influenced the writing of this book that it would be impossible to recognize them all. However, I feel compelled to mention the following:

To the many individuals who attended my classes, seminars, and talks. You gave me insights, made suggestions, and encouraged me to write, and I owe each of you a debt of gratitude.

To Chuck Farnsworth because of your loyal friendship, for "jump starting" me many years ago in Binghamton, New York, and for writing the foreword.

To Stewart Marston because you were the catalyst that really got me moving. In addition, your technical skills, advice, book cover art and patience have been invaluable. Thanks for showing up in my life.

To all my canine friends, Ellie, Tig, Danny, and to my faithful hunting dogs, Buck, Pepper, Geet, and Annie for helping me stay sane.

And finally, to Shirley, my wife, who has been a bedrock with her kindness, patience, and unwavering support, a big hug and a huge "thanks".

About the Author

Bill holds both a B.S. and M.S. from the University of Tennessee in Knoxville. In 1966 after completing Officer's Candidate School, Bill was commissioned as an officer in the Marine Corps. He served thirteen months in South Vietnam and was honorably discharged in 1969 as a Captain.

The majority of his professional career was spent working at Columbia State Community College where he served in various positions. Currently he is taking his life experiences to a deeper level as he continues to facilitate "Principles of Effectiveness" for both individuals and organizations.

Bill and his wife Shirley live in the small rural community of Duck River, Tennessee where they reside on their family farm.

CPSIA information can be obtained at www.ICGtesting.com
Printed in the USA
LVOW100614030212

266881LV00001B/4/P